ISBN 978-1-5277-0590-6
PIBN 10882805

1 MONTH OF
FREE
READING

at

www.ForgottenBooks.com

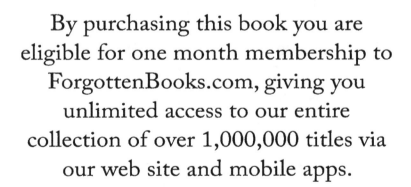

By purchasing this book you are eligible for one month membership to ForgottenBooks.com, giving you unlimited access to our entire collection of over 1,000,000 titles via our web site and mobile apps.

To claim your free month visit:

www.forgottenbooks.com/free882805

English
Français
Deutsche
Italiano
Español
Português

www.forgottenbooks.com

Mythology Photography **Fiction**
Fishing Christianity **Art** Cooking
Essays Buddhism Freemasonry
Medicine **Biology** Music **Ancient**
Egypt Evolution Carpentry Physics
Dance Geology **Mathematics** Fitness
Shakespeare **Folklore** Yoga Marketing
Confidence Immortality Biographies
Poetry **Psychology** Witchcraft
Electronics Chemistry History **Law**
Accounting **Philosophy** Anthropology
Alchemy Drama Quantum Mechanics
Atheism Sexual Health **Ancient History**
Entrepreneurship Languages Sport
Paleontology Needlework Islam
Metaphysics Investment Archaeology
Parenting Statistics Criminology
Motivational

The Bells of Old
St. Paul's

By
Theodosia Wales Glenn

The celebration of the fiftieth year of the rectorship of Rev. Robert Brent Drane, D.D., and portraying some incidents in the famous history of old St. Paul's Parish, Edenton, N. C., being the 225th year of the founding of the Parish.

To be staged in St. Paul's Churchyard at the foot of the old belfry on All Saints' Day, November 1, 1926.

REV. ROBERT BRENT DRANE, D.D
Rector of St. Paul's Church
Edenton, N. C.

ST. PAUL'S CHURCH, EDENTON, N. C.

PROLOGUE
By the Spirit of Old St. Paul's.

SODE I:

THE FAR-AWAY BELL OF THE EARLY SETTLERS: ORGANIZATION OF THE FIRST VESTRY OF ST. PAUL'S, THE OLDEST CORPORATION IN NORTH CAROLINA—
DECEMBER 15, 1701.

SODE II:

FROM TOM TOM TO SCHOOL BELL: THE CHIEF OF THE CHOWANOKE INDIANS BRINGS HIS SON TO THE PARISH SCHOOL LOCATED AT SARUM. 1712.

SODE III:

THE BELL OF PIOUS DEVOTION: THE PRESENTATION OF THE CHALICE AND PATEN TO ST. PAUL'S CHURCH BY COL. EDWARD MOSELY. 1725.

SODE IV:

THE BELL OF INDEPENDENCE: THE SIGNING OF THE TEST BY THE VESTRY OF ST. PAUL'S, JUNE 19, 1776.

SODE V:

THE BELL BATTERY: ST. PAUL'S BELL IS MELTED INTO CANNON. A FAREWELL TO MOTHERS AND SWEETHEARTS. 1861.

ODE VI:

ARMISTICE BELLS THAT PEALED FOR A WAR-FREE WORLD. NOVEMBER 11, 1918.

ODE VII:

JUBILEE BELLS, VOICING THE NOTE OF HONORED ACHIEVEMENT—
NOVEMBER 1, 1926.

SODE VII:

THE GOLDEN BELLS BEYOND ST. PAUL'S CHURCHYARD.

4

PROLOGUE

Choir (within the church):

> Far, far away like bells at evening pealing,
> The voice of Jesus sounds o'er land and sea;
> And laden souls by thousands meekly stealing,
> Kind Shepherd, turn their weary steps to Thee.
>> Angels of Jesus, angels of ig ,
>> Singing to welcome the pilgrims of the night.

St. Paul's bell rings as for early morning devotions.

Dr. Drane enters and pauses, looking up at the belfry. He speaks:

"Old Bell, if you could but once unloose that brazen tongue and tell of all that ever has transpired within the shadow of this tower, if our eyes could once behold all those who e'er have passed within these portals, what a varied pageant would be now unrolled."

Exit.

Now speaks the Spirit of Old St. Paul's—a voice from the belfry:

> Listening long in misty bell tower
> Through sunny peace and war's dun glower,
> Ripe in time's grey wisdom hoary,
> Edenton's long checkered story,
> Through the slow years' soft footfalls
> Stands the Spirit of St. Paul's.
>
> Watch it keeps, and that unceasing
> Through the ripe years slow increasing,
> Watch o'er childhood's careless laughter,
> Watch o'er dull care following after,
> Watch o'er baby's sweet baptism,
> Watch o'er patriots' crimson vision,
> Watch o'er bright gay wedding bell,

5

Watch o'er death's slow leaden knell,
Watch o'er pain's long midnight vigil,
Summer's sun and winter's bleak chill.
Watch o'er vows to God and Heaven,
O'er those who for the right have striven:
Watch of St. Paul's cross-crowned spire—
Holy watch that ne'er shall tire.

Dawneth now our blessed Saints' Day,
Day when hearts are filled with hope's ray,
Day when spirits dear from Heaven
Who from us by death were riven,
Drawn by human hearts' keen hunger,
Those whom Death himself can't sunder,
Near to earth's loved spots will hover:
Mother, son, the maid and lover
Back to old St. Paul's will come
And linger here till setting sun.

Hark the bell in belfry tower,
Golden notes like sun on shower,
As a harp in tune with nature
Reverberates with Heaven's rapture,
As a heart that loves unstinted
Gathers melodies scarce hinted,
So the old bell's gathered story
Pealeth forth in tones of glory:
Story of past generations,
All the soul's deep venerations;
Childhood, youth and then ripe old age,
Bashful lovers, fools and wise sage,
Sleep at last in the old Churchyard,
O'er their graves the mossy greensward,
Children still to old St. Paul's.

Summoned by the voice of that one
Who shall hear the Master's "Well done,"
Who St. Paul's long years hath guarded,
All its treasures safely hoarded,
Served with love that knows no measure,
St. Paul's weal his greatest pleasure,
Who hath cherished all her history,
Charmed with all her sacred mystery,
Footsteps of her daughters guided,
With the right hath ever sided,
Sent forth sons with mission zeal
Who the world's deep woe can feel,
To blazon cross from palm to snow field,
(For only in the cross is sin healed)—
When her record now he'd seek,
St. Paul's Spirit needs must speak.
Hush then your beating hearts so eager,
And your faith must not be meager;
Summoned by the bell's soft pealing
From dim past they now come stealing,
Soft their voices gently humming,
You can see them coming, coming,
Trooping back to old St. Paul's.

First of all the settlers early,
Braving dangers dark and surly,
Those who summoned her to being,
Their new country's weal foreseeing,
Carolina's oldest Vestry,
Wrote their names in lasting history,
Builders of the first St. Paul's.

EPISODE I.
THE BELL OF THE EARLY SETTLERS

A distant bell rings.

Entrance music by choir "Faith of Our Fathers."

Enter a group of men, the twelve members of the first Vestry, and others.

Gov. Henderson Walker: We are gathered here, my friends, to organize our Vestry, the first religious corporation in the vast wilderness of Carolina. The following having been appointed by the General Assembly as members of this Vestry, I will now proceed to call the roll. Gov. Henderson Walker, Col. Thomas Pollock, William Duckinfield, Nicholas Crisp, Edward Smithwick, John Blount, Jas. Long, Nathaniel Chevin, William Benbury, Col. William Wilkinson, Capt. Thos. Leuten, Capt. Thomas Blount.

As these names are called the characters step forward and respond.

Gov. Walker: "What nominations do we hear for officers of the Vestry?"

John Blount: "I nominate Col. William Wilkinson for Senior Warden."

Wm. Duckinfield: "I second the motion."

Gov. Walker: "The motion has been made and seconded; all in favor make it known by saying 'aye,' all opposed, 'no.' Col. William Wilkinson is duly elected Senior Warden of our Vestry. Nomination for Junior Warden is now in order."

William Benbury: "I nominate Capt. Thomas Leuten for Junior Warden of the Vestry."

Thos. Pollock: "I second the motion."

Gov. Walker: "The motion has been made and seconded; all in favor make it known by saying 'aye', all opposed, 'no.' Capt. Thos. Leuten is duly elected Junior War-

8

den of our Vestry. In behalf of the Vestry, I hereby appoint Richard Churton as Lay Reader for this Parish of St. Pau.'s. We wi. now proceed to consider the matter of a location and building for a church."

Edward Smithwick: "I offer to give one acre of land on my old plantation and a conveyance of same to the church wardens."

Col. Pollock: "I move that the wardens shall agree with the workmen for the building of a church twenty-five feet long with posts in the ground."

The men with the four logs move forward and stand these posts upright in a square, and all gather about and sing "How Firm a Foundation." At the close of this all bow their heads while the Lay Reader pronounces the benediction.

Exeunt.

EPISODE II.
FROM TOM TOM TO SCHOOL BELL.
Spirit of St. Paul's.

From the Little River waters,
From the cool deep forest fastness,
Come the red skins, Chowanookas,
Come to bring the Chief's son, Powtook,
Here to learn the white man's wisdom,
Join the Masburn School at Sarum.
Come the brave chiefs bearing tokens

Of their love for friendly white man,
Come the squaws and small papooses
With their gifts of baskets, blankets,
Come and gather for a blessing
At the hands of the White Father;
And the tom-tom falls to silence
At the silver tone of school bell.

9

The parish missionary, Mr. Rainsford, enters, accompanied by the teacher, Mr. Masburn, and several boys carrying books. The Indian Chief and his son with several braves, squaws and children enter, bringing gifts.

Music by choir, "By the Waters of the Minnetonka." Indians kneel before priest, then the hand of the Chief's son is placed in that of the teacher and Indians exeunt to beat of tomtom. As school bell rings in the distance, the tom-tom ceases and Indians pause in listening attitude, then pass off stage.

EPISODE III.
THE BELL OF PIOUS DEVOTION.

The Bell of St. Paul's rings as for Sabbath worship.
Spirit of St. Paul's:
The days of chivalry had scarcely waned,
The legend of the Grail still held its sway
O'er knightly hearts of earnest men.
But none could say as did the holy maid
Of Arthur's day,
"Sweet brother, I have seen the Holy Grail,
For waked at dead of night I heard a sound
As of a silver horn from o'er the hills,
As from a distance beyond distance grew
Coming upon me—Oh, never harp nor horn
Nor aught we blow with breath or touch with hand
Was like that music as it came and then
Streamed through my cell a cold and silver beam,
And down the long beam stole the Holy Grail
Rose red with beatings in it as if alive
Till all the white walls of my cell were dyed
With rosy colors leaping on the wall,
And then the music passed."*

While none could say as did that maid.
The Holy Thing is here, I've seen it,—Still.
*With acknowledgment to Tennyson's "Holy Grail."

10

There came one from the English shores,—a man
Within whose heart there burned a holy fire;
A man of soldier mein and knightly heart,
And oft he thought on Christ and his dear love,
The body broken for us, the shed blood—
And in his heart the purpose grew
That this first church in Carolina
Should have a chalice all of silver pure
And therewithal a paten for the broken bread,
And—lest children reared in wilderness
Should brutish grow and ignorant,
He added to his gift some mighty tomes,
Provincial library for the colony.
These gifts he brought to Edenton,
The greatest township then of Carolina,
And bowing low at St. Paul's door
His gifts he offered to the village priest,
And as his heart was lifted in rapt thought
A heavenly melody did fill his soul
And on his inner vision flashed the Grail.

Entrance music, "And Now O Father, Mindful of Thy Love," by choir. Enter parish missionary, John Blacknall and Col. Edward Mosely, followed by group of boys carrying leather-bound volumes. Col. Mosely kneels at the feet of Blacknall, presenting the chalice; Blacknall lifts the chalice high, while Mosely continues to hold the paten with face uplifted toward the chalice. Music, Grail Motif from "Parsifal." At the close of this the choir sings "Bread of the World in Mercy Broken," while Col. Mosely and the boys rise from their knees and follow the priest into the church.

EPISODE IV.
THE INDEPENDENCE BELL*

Voice from the Belfry:

There is tumult in the village,

*With acknowledgments to Longfellow's "Independence Bell."

11

In our quaint old Edenton,
And the streets are rife with people
Pacing restless up and down,
People gathering at corners
Where they whisper each to each,
And the sweat stands on their temples
With the earnestness of speech.

And they gather now at St. Paul's
Where the Vestry meets today;
The Test will be propounded
And each man will have his say.
"Will they do it"? "Dare they do it"?
"Who'll be speaking"? "What's the news"?
"What of Hoskins"? "What of Benbury"?
"Oh, God grant they won't refuse."

See, see, the dense crowd quiver,
For there coming in the gate
Are Roberts, Rice and Beasley,
On their action hangs our fate.
Read it now, the declaration,
For the women had their say
At the Edenton Tea Party,
Claim from England now fair play.

'Tis a time of agitation
And our liberty's at stake,
If the Vestry pass this measure
War will follow in its wake.
How they'll shout then, what a tumult,
How the old bell then will snarl
Till the clang of freedom ruffles
The calm gliding Albemarle.

12

Hushed the people's swelling murmur,
Thomas Benbury will read
Give us time men in the Vestry
Earnest thinking's what we need.
If we pass it, you shall know i'
For Old St. Paul's bell will speak
And liberty re-echo .
Maine to Gulf and Chesapeake.

The crowd enters and surges around the foot of the
tower, looking up at the belfry and then at the vestrymen
as they enter. A group of Tories draw to one side, as if
plotting together. There are cries of "Let's hear it now,"
"the Test! the Test!" Thos. Benbury steps up on the ele-
vation, "Here it is, Edenton citizens, the rough draft. 'Tis
but fitting you should share it before the Vestry acts." He
reads the Test.
.   We, the subscribers, professing our allegiance to the
king and acknowledging the constitutional executive power
of government, do solemnly profess, testify and declare that
we do absolutely believe that neither the Parliament of
Great Britain nor any member or constituent branch thereof
have a right to impose taxes upon these colonies to regulate
the internal policy thereof, and that all attempts by fraud
or force to establish and exercise such claims and powers
are violations of the peace and security of the people and
ought to be resisted to the utmost, and that the people of
this province, singly and collectively, are bound by the acts
and resolutions of the continental and provincial congresses,
because in both they are fully represented by persons chosen
by themselves, and we do solemnly and sincerely promise
and engage under the sanction of virtue, honor and sacred
Love of Liberty and our country to maintain and support all

and every the acts, resolutions and regulations of the said Continental and Provincial Congresses to the utmost of our power and ability. In testimony whereof we have hereto set our hands, this 19th day of June, 1776.

(Signers):

Richard Hoskins
David Rice
Pelatiah Walton
Wm. Hinton
Thos. Bonner
Wm. Boyd
Thos. Benbury
Jacob Hunter
John Beasley
Wm. Bennet
William Roberts

Mrs. Penelope Barker: "The women have already taken their stand. At a tea-party at Mrs. Elizabeth King's, where tea was conspicuous for its absence, a resolution was drawn up and signed by every woman present in which we swore to drink no more tea until the odious tax is removed. Edenton women will back the Vestry if they pass the Test."

Mrs. Winifred Hoskins: "And our men needn't call on us to serve them good things if they do not prove as valiant as the ladies in times like these.

An old man wearing a knitted cap touches his cap and says, "You all know how I lost my scalp as a boy in that famous Indian raid. They say the Red Coats are stirring up the Indian tribes. There will be war and a fierce one, but I am ready." He grips his gun.

An old Tory: "Fie upon you, men! One regiment of well trained regulars from England can soon wipe out all the bob-tail, hit-or-miss parcel you can muster in this colony.

14

I'll not hear the King's cause defamed. The King himself shall learn of this."

A man in the crowd: "Let him hear about it. We are no craven cowards."

Tory: "Dogs!" He stalks out, followed by the little group of men with whom he has been talking.

The vestrymen pass into the church. A boy posts himself as if on guard at the doorway. Someone points to him. and a man says "Yes, the boy is to give the signal to the bell-ringer if the Test is passed."

There is a tense silence as if the people are awed by a realization of the import of the moment. A murmur within as if the Vestry are at prayer. There are bowed heads without.

Suddenly the boy straightens up and touches his cap. "Make way there," he says, and running he pushes his way through the crowd to the foot of the belfry. "Ring, bell-man," he shouts, "Ring! Oh, ring for liberty!"

The clamor of the bells is mingled with the hurrahs of the people. People embrace one another and show great feeling. The vestrymen have rejoined the crowd and lead the exit while the crowd sings "Yankee Doodle."

EPISODE V.

THE BELL BATTERY.

The bell of St. Paul's rings as for Vespers. A group gathers for the service. A young man in grey uniform, pausing with his sweetheart's arm in his, looks up at the belfry and says, "I wonder if I will ever again hear that old bell ring out over St. Paul's Churchyard."

A girl dressed in period of 1861 mounts the platform and recites

MELT THE BELLS.

Melt the bells, melt the bells;
Still the tinkling on the plain
And transmute the evening chimes
Into war's resounding rhymes,
That invaders may be slain
   By the bells.

Melt the bells, melt the bells,
That for years have called to prayer,
And instead the cannon's roar
Shall resound the valley o'er,
That the foe may catch despair
   From the bells.

Melt the bells, melt the bells;
Though it cost a tear to part
With the music they have made,
Where the friends we love are laid
With pale cheek and silent heart
   'Neath the bells.

Melt the bells, melt the bells·
Into cannon vast and grim,
And the foe shall feel the ire
From their heaving lungs of fire,
And we'll put our trust in Him
   And the bells.

Melt the bells, melt the bells;
And when foes no more attack,
And the lightning cloud of war
Shall roll thunderless and far,
We will melt the cannon back
   Into bells.

Melt the bells, melt the bells;
And they'll peal a sweeter chime,
And remind of all the brave
Who have sunk to glory's grave.
And will sleep thro' coming time
'Neath the bells.

As this is recited a curtain is pulled back from across upper
stage, disclosing silhouette of a cannon against a lurid sky.
Choir sings a verse of "The Soldier's Farewell." There is pan-
tomine of parting, waving of handkerchiefs, etc. This is in-
terrupted by note of fife and drum playing "Dixie" and boys in
grey fall into line and march off. All wave till boys are out of
sight. As they fall into line, one young girl may run out and
throw her arms around her lover, then tear herself away
Exeunt, going in different directions, many into the church.

EPISODE VI.
ARMISTICE BELLS.

Spirit of St. Paul's:
IN FLANDERS FIELD

In Flanders field the poppies blow
Between the crosses row on row
That mark our place, and in the sky
The larks still bravely singing, fly,
Scarce heard amid the guns below.

We are the Dead; short days ago
We lived, felt dawn, saw sunset glow,
Loved and were loved, and now we lie
In Flanders field.

Take up our quarrel with the foe:
To you from failing hands we throw the torch.
Be yours to hold it high:
If you break faith with us who die

17

We shall not sleep, though poppies grow
In Flanders field.

(John McCrae)

The black draped figure of Humanity kneels with hands out-stretched toward silhouette of crosses on Flanders field, black against a leaden sky. As the reading closes the choir sings soft-ly "There's a Long, Long Trail A-Winding." Stretcher bearers enter stage left carrying wounded soldier attended by Red Cross nurse. They pause stage center to minister to the wounded man. The music changes to "Oh, Come Ye Disconsolate," Dr. Drane appears at the church door and the wounded man is car-ried in. A golden star gleams out above the church door.

The choir sings (to the tune of "All Hail, Immanuel.")

All hail to thee, glad Armistice,
The war-torn world acclaims thee,
And weary hearts throughout the earth
With thy glad bells from gloom set free,
Sing praise to God who giveth peace
And causeth war's mad hell to cease,
Now echo back the mighty song,
Yea, peal, yea, peal, yea, peal, yea, peal, for Armistice.
Peal for Armistice, for Armistice,
Peal for Armistice, for Armistice,
Battle, fire, and cannon's roar,
Hushed by the peace our hearts implore
Peace for evermore.
Peal for armistice, for armistice,
Peal for armistice, for armistice,
Prince of Peace and Lord of Lords,
All praise for armistice.

As this is sung the figure of Humanity rises slowly, throws back her black garments, disclosing a radiant figure clad in white with a glistening cross on her breast, and the scene changes to a silhouette of golden crosses against a sky of blue, Old St. Paul's bell peals out the glad news of the Armistice.

EPISODE VII.
JUBILEE BELLS.

Voicing the note of honored achievement. The precious web of memory is woven in which may be distinguished the cross that crowns the belfry.

Sung by choir within (to the tune of "Oh, Mother Dear Jerusalem.")

DEAR OLD ST. PAUL'S

Oh, beautiful for garnered sheaves
Thy bounteous sowings yield,
Through sunshine's glow,
Through sleet and snow,
In many a distant field.
Dear old St. Paul's, dear old St. Paul's,
Thy sons have sallied forth
To tell the news of Christ's dear love
From palms to frozen north.

O beautiful for sacrifice,
The men who reared thy walls,
Who preached the gospel fearlessly
Within its sacred halls.
Dear old St. Paul's, dear old St. Paul's,
God's grace to thee is given
In one great soul who long hath stood
To point our way to Heaven.

Oh, beautiful for service true,
With gentle mein and kind,
Where love for God and love for man
Blend in one heart and mind.
Dear old St. Paul's, dear old St. Paul's,
God shed His grace on thee,

19

Still grant that he
Long years may be
Our messenger from Thee.

(With acknowledgments to Miss Katherine Lee Bates, author of "America, the Beautiful.")

Spirit of St. Paul's:

A PSALM OF LIFE.

(With acknowledgments to Longfellow's "Psalm of Life.")

Tell us not, oh, pealing church bell,
Life is but an empty dream,
For the best is yet before us,
Onward beckoning with its gleam.

But the past has still its message
Weaves the fabric which the soul
Must wear, its wedding garment,
While eternity shall roll.

On All Saints' Day at St. Paul's
Can the Spirit in the bell
Call the souls of those who love her
Back to us their tale to tell?

Come, ye children of St. Paul's
From the earliest day till now,
Gather now and weave the pattern,
St. Paul's message, sacred vow.

Weave a fabric far more precious
Than the treasured Golden Fleece,
Checkered pattern, like a sampler,
Gray and golden, war and peace.

In and out then, back and forth,
Footsteps through these sacred halls,
Like a shuttle weave the tissue,
Memory's web for old St. Paul's.

But now, mark ye, 'mid the colors,
Howe'er mingled, through all time,
Shines the cross that crowns our belfry,
Cross of Christ with head sublime.

Only as that cross is inwrought
In the tissue of our lives
Can we know the hallowed meaning,
The truth for which old St. Paul's strives.

See the blue of loyal-hearted
Men who built the old St. Paul's,
Red of Indian, white of Chalice,
Souls made pure from stain of fall.

In the heat of Revolution
All these strands, red, white and blue,
By the Test are interwoven,
A fit emblem for the true.

Then the gray of that thin front line
Held for years against the foe,
While the melted bells did thunder
And loving hearts were bleeding so.

Find the olive drab of World War,
Millions lying 'neath the cross

That the war against all warfare
May not end in mankind's loss.

Find at last the glowing colors
Of the ripened golden grain,
Golden deeds that crown his service,
Loving homage, Dr. Drane.

Love for children, bridal parties.
Deeds of kindness, building plans,
Consolation, Christian nurture
Built on rock, enduring stands.

In a holy zeal for missions
St. Paul's Spirit ventures forth
To tell the old, old story
From sunlit palm to frozen north.

And the victor's laurel chaplet
Should with years his brow adorn,
But he treadeth in the footprints
Of Him who wore the crown of thorn.

So Humanity is summoned
Whom he's served these fifty years,
Love for God and love for mankind,
Rain and sunshine, joy and tears.

In a cherished casket garnered,
Not a fabled treasure-trove,
But a symbol of devotion,
A simple token of our love.

And Humanity shall bear it,
Lay our small gift at his feet,
Know that no small earthly present
Could our love for him complete.

Gleams the cross in memory's fabric,
Like the shining of the sun,
He hath wrought in noble pattern,
List, the Master's glad "Well done."

Lives of great men all remind us
We should make our lives sublime,
And departing leave behind us
Footprints on the sands of time.

At the conclusion of this Psalm of Life the choir sings "Lead
on. Oh, King Eternal," and there commences a processional of
the pageant participants, Dr. Drane leading and taking his place
at stage center. The characters from first six tableaux wind in
and out and take their stand on either side, leaving center of
stage open for personifications of Dr. Drane's labors of love—
little children carrying flowers to scatter at his feet, bridal par-
ties, the widow in her weeds, Sunday School children with Bibles
and Prayer Books, and some representatives of the fruits of mis-
sionary endeavor, native Christians from several countries in
costume.

When all have assembled there is a change in the music to
the Spinning Song and the pageant participants weave in and
out as indicated in words to the Psalm of Life, until just below
Dr. Drane there appears the Web of Memory, in which may be
discerned the golden gleaming of a cross. Above on the belfry
a cross shines out.

EPISODE VIII.
THE GOLDEN BELLS BEYOND OLD ST. PAUL'S CHURCHYARD.

While tableau seven is still posed, the soloist within the
church sings "When They Ring the Golden Bells For You and
Me." As this is sung a group of angel trumpeters appear in the

23

background, with trumpets uplifted, and hold this position until close of pageant.

Then the music changes to,

Far, far away like bells at evening pealing
The voice of Jesus sounds o'er land and sea,
And laden souls by thousands meekly stealing
Kind Shepherd, turn their weary steps to Thee.

Angels of Jesus, Angels of light,
Singing to welcome the pilgrims of the night.

FINIS.

zabeth
ɒduke.edu

DECENNIAL CELEBRATION

OF THE

ORGANIZATION OF KINGS MOUNTAIN PRESBYTERY.

LINCOLNTON, NORTH CAROLINA

NOVEMBER 12TH, 13TH, 1912.

The Tenth Anniversary of the organization of Kings Mountain Presbytery was celebrated in the Presbyterian church in Lincolnton, November the 12th and 13th. The Presbytery of Kings Mountain was organized in Lincolnton, November the 18th 1902. It was set off from Mecklenburg Presbytery and composed of the five counties of Lincoln, Gaston, Cleveland, Rutherford and Polk. An interesting programme had been arranged for the occasion by the committee having the matter in charge.

An invitation had been extended to all the churches of the Presbytery to send delegates, and the occasion was pleasant and profitable to those who attended. The exercises were presided over with ease and grace by Rev Geo. A. Sparrow, to whose preparation of the programme and persistent effort much of the credit for the successful celebration is due.

Tuesday evening the exercises were opened by an address of welcome by Elder A. M. Hoke of Lincolnton; response, P. W. Garland, Esq., of Gastonia, which was followed by an address outlining the history of Presbyterianism to the formation of Kings Mountain Presbytery by Elder A. Nixon.

Wednesday morning Rev. R. A. Miller discussed the subject, "Has Kings Mountain Presbytery justified the action of Synod in the separation." Rev. S. L. Cathey read a Memorial of the deceased Brethren —charter members. Touching remarks were made by a number of the delegates on the lives, character and works of the departed.

Wednesday afternoon from 2 p. m. until 7:30 p. m. was devoted to social intercourse. The ladies entertained the delegates and the congregation at a reception in the Confederate Memorial Hall. The hours spent in this interesting old Hall were delightfully passed and will be long treasured.

Wednesday evening Rev. W. E. McIlwaine of Charlotte in felicitous words brought greetings and congratulations from the mother

CPSIA information can be obtained
at www.ICGtesting.com
Printed in the USA
BVHW091507191118
533509BV00029B/3261/P

9 781527 705906